PET OWNER'S GUIDE TO THE
CAIRN TERRIER

Ron & Brenda Birch

RINGPRESS

ABOUT THE AUTHORS

Ron and Brenda Birch have been involved with Cairn Terriers for nearly thirty years, breeding, showing under their highly successful Kinkim prefix, as well as judging at Championship level. During their time in the breed they have made up nine Champions, and they have won Best of Breed at Crufts for three consecutive years. Their most successful dog, Ch. Kinkim Ludvic, has won 34 Challenge Certificates, two Best in Show awards at General Championship Shows, and he is the only Cairn Terrier to have reached the final six at Crufts.

Both Ron and Brenda have served on the Southern Cairn Terrier Club committee for many years – Ron has been treasurer since 1981 and chairman since 1988. He writes a weekly column in the canine press.

Brenda has edited the Club Year Book since 1984; she is the Cairn Terrier breed historian, and is one of the three founder members of Cairn Terrier Health Watch.

Photography: Sheila Atter.

Published by Ringpress Books Limited,
PO Box 8, Lydney, Gloucestershire,
GL15 4YN, United Kingdom.

First published 1999
©1999 Ringpress Books Limited. All rights reserved

ISBN 1 86054 111 9

Printed in Hong Kong

CONTENTS

Introducing The Cairn Terrier

The Cairn Terrier is a lively, energetic, intelligent small dog, who should look alert and ready for anything. He is small enough to be picked up and carried, but tough enough to have a good romp or a long walk, both of which he enjoys. He should weigh between 6-7.5 kgs (14-16 lbs) and stand 28-31 cms (11-12 ins) at the shoulder. He is not trimmed into an unnatural shape, although he should be sufficiently groomed to avoid looking shabby. Although the Cairn is small, there is nothing 'toyish' about him, either in looks or in physique. He is quick to learn, bright and plucky, but not quarrelsome. These attributes were essential for his ancestors' continued existence for hundreds of years as working terriers in the Highlands and Islands of Scotland.

A Cairn loves the company of humans and will be devoted to his family. He is usually friendly and confident, but may be quite cool with strangers. He is adaptable enough to live in a town, in a country home or on a farm. Wherever he lives, he will enjoy being taken for a walk. Exercise keeps his mind and body active and to deny it would make him sluggish.

When taken for a walk, not only is the trotting helpful as physical exercise, but the sniffing and smelling is the dog's way of communicating and helps to keep his mind active. All breeds of dog sniff and smell each other – this is their 'conversation'.

BORN TO DIG

The word terrier means 'earth dog'. The Cairn is a true terrier, born to dig, and, although only a small dog, he is able to move an amazing amount of soil in a short time. He can, of course, be trained not to dig in flowerbeds but digging comes naturally to him

Friendly and confident, the Cairn Terrier will adapt to both town and country living.

and is excellent exercise. If you are a very keen gardener and your garden is your pride and joy, it would be better not to have a Cairn.

Indeed it may be better to have no dog at all, for most breeds dig at times; it is one of their inborn instincts to dig a hole for a nest.

HISTORY

The Cairn is not a man-made breed; he evolved naturally over hundreds of years in the Highlands and Islands of Scotland. His ancestors were kept to hunt and kill vermin. Each Scottish laird had his own 'cullach de madaidhean' (pack of

Cairn Terriers portrayed in a painting by F.T. Daws, 1934.
Reproduced from Hutchinsons Dog Encyclopaedia.
Photo: Carol Ann Johnson.

dogs), and crofters had their own 'madah' (house-dog).

In the 15th century, Bishop Lesley of Ross wrote of a "dog of low height which, creeping into subterraneous burrows, routs out foxes, badgers, martens and wild cats from their lurking places and dens; and if he finds the passage too narrow, opens himself a way with his feet, and that with so great labour that he frequently perishes through his own exertions". He was surely describing the ancestors of the present-day Cairn. In those distant days, the Cairn would be kept for his working ability, and, if any matings were arranged, this working ability would be the only consideration.

Several of the terriers of Scotland – Dandie Dinmont, Skye, Scottish and West Highland White – have supporters who claim that their breed is the aboriginal terrier of Scotland. It is quite probable that the different varieties originated in different areas of the country. In the far distant days, no records were kept, and so this cannot be proven.

In the UK, The Kennel Club was formed in 1873, and records started to be kept. In the early part of the 20th century, there

INTRODUCING THE CAIRN TERRIER

was much discussion and disagreement about the name for the breed, but eventually 'Cairn Terrier' was agreed. In 1911, a Standard of points for the Cairn Terrier was drawn up, and this was a basis for the present-day Standard by which Cairns are judged. It was quite common for Cairns and West Highland White Terriers to be interbred until the

The Cairn Terrier may not resemble its ancestor the wolf, but it still displays behavioural traits that are part of every domestic dog's inheritance. Photo: McGovern.

Kennel Club passed a resolution in 1924 stating that, as from January 1st 1925, they should be two distinct breeds.

The American Kennel club was formed in 1884. While it is thought that Cairn-type dogs were in the USA in the early years of the 20th century, it was not until 1913 that documentation shows Cairns being imported into the country. In 1917, the American Kennel Club took action to bar any Cairn from registration if it was a Cairn and West Highland White Terrier cross.

THE WOLF'S LEGACY

All dogs have approximately 95 per cent wolf DNA, and therefore much of their behaviour is wolf-like: the constant wish to be 'top dog' in the pack; the ritual greeting; territory marking; the predatory instinct that makes all dogs keen to chase their prey. These traits can be seen in all dogs; they are inborn and cannot be altered. You will easily notice them in your Cairn. He will become top dog if you allow him to. He will greet you enthusiastically, even if you have only been away for a short time. He will mark his territory with a few drops of urine mixed with a

The pack mentality is very strong in every canine.

secretion from the preputial glands when out for a walk, to inform other canines that he has walked that way. He will chase a ball, and may chase a cat or a squirrel. If he is in the company of another dog, or dogs, they form a 'pack', however small, and will chase other animals. This can lead them into trouble and you may be fined for any damage caused. Although Cairns can live on manufactured foods, his wolf's digestive tract, which was designed to eat meat and green matter, has not altered.

Generations of breeding and rearing puppies with humans have controlled these instincts to a certain degree, but they are still there.

2 Cairn Characteristics

There are people who think that a Cairn would be a suitable dog for them because they have read that he is a small dog with a coat that does not need a lot of grooming. This is quite true, but it must be realised that he is a much more active dog than many larger breeds; he can out-run most of them, and has more general intelligence. There are several things to think about before deciding to have a Cairn.

BASIC QUESTIONS

Are you a suitable owner, prepared to spend time and money to look after him? A Cairn is not merely a possession to be fed and watered but a lively, intelligent creature. Are you prepared to exercise him? It is possible for a Cairn to live without long walks every day, but he should have as much exercise as possible. Do you wish to have him for a friend for the next 12 to 15 years? A Cairn needs, and thrives

on, companionship and love. Are you legally allowed to have a dog? Whether you own your home or not, make sure that there is nothing in any agreement to prevent you having a dog. Is someone at home most of the day? A Cairn is not a dog who will sit around and do nothing all day. Where is the Cairn to sleep? It is not a good idea to allow him to sleep on your bed, because, if you have to go away at any time, he will fret if he is used to you being there. What do you plan to do with excreta? A chemical doggy loo, which is dug into the ground and all excreta dropped into it, is successful if properly used.

What about holidays? You may not wish, or be able, to take your Cairn on holiday with you. If that is so, you will have to make arrangements for him to be looked after. You may be able to arrange for someone to stay in your home, or you may have a friend or

This is a breed that thrives on human companionship, and should not be left on its own for long periods.

relative who would look after him in their home. You may put him in boarding kennels, but they vary a great deal and are expensive. What are you going to do with him if you have to go somewhere that he cannot go? There will surely come a time when you have to go out for a few hours or for an evening. You have a Cairn when it is convenient and also when it is inconvenient. He should have been brought up to be sensible enough to be left for two to three hours without barking, whining or making a fuss, but, for a longer time, it will be necessary for someone to attend to him.

Is the garden Cairn-proof? A Cairn can escape through unbelievably small holes or dig his way under a fence, and some can jump over gates that are 4 feet (1.25 metres) high.

You should never buy a Cairn puppy because the children want one. It is quite natural for children to want a puppy, but they cannot take the responsibility of a living animal and no one should expect them to. A Cairn should never be bought in the same way as the latest toy; the children may love him very much, and he may become their best friend, but they are not mature enough to be accountable for decisions that will have to be taken. The adult members of the family must want a dog, and must be prepared to look after him, physically, mentally and financially, for all of his life. During that time, the children will probably leave home.

COSTS

Can you afford the food, the vet's bills and maybe to pay someone to look after him if you have to go out? The cost of everything is rising, and likely to go on doing so. A Cairn is not an expensive dog to keep – an adult keeps fit and well on quite a small amount of food. Vet's bills are expensive, and although, as a breed, Cairns normally keep free of ailments, this cannot be guaranteed. Any living creature may become ill.

MALE OR FEMALE?

Some people have definite thoughts on whether to have a male or a female, but for others it can be difficult to decide. It may be thought that a female is more

Personality varies between individuals, so whether you choose a male or a female is a matter of personal choice.

CAIRN COLOURS

Wheaten.

Red brindle.

CAIRN COLOURS

Red.

Grey brindle.

friendly than a male, but this is not necessarily so, as temperaments are individual.

SEASONAL CYCLE
Female puppies can come in season at about six months of age, but it is often later. Unless she is neutered, a bitch will have twice-yearly seasons, and will need to be confined for three to four weeks during her seasons. This can be difficult if there are several children in the household, who may forget to close doors properly.

MALE CHARACTERISTICS
The age at which a male puppy 'lifts his leg' also varies. Unless a dog is neutered, he will go in search of any bitch in season. This is normal and natural, and should be taken into consideration before buying.

Some people say they do not wish to have a male because he may mount cushions, legs or arms. This can happen if a dog is bored, does not receive any mental or physical exercise or is left alone for long periods of time. It is possible that he could be mentally below par, but it is very rare to find a Cairn that is not sensible.

If mounting should occur, it should be stopped immediately.

Never turn a blind eye and hope he will grow out of it. Say "No!" in a loud, horrified voice, pick him up very firmly and put him in the garden or somewhere by himself, shut the door on him and leave him alone for ten to fifteen minutes. Do not put him in his bed, or wherever he lives; they are places he should associate with normal living and pleasure. Completely ignore the incident when you let him back in – do not say anything silly, such as "who was a naughty boy, then?"

Do not think that if your dog mates a bitch it will satisfy him! It will not – he will immediately want to mate another.

It is not a good idea to allow a pet male Cairn to be used as a stud dog. Some are quite happy to return to their normal lifestyle after mating a bitch, but some will persist in lifting their leg and making their mark with a few drops of urine. This is their way of telling any other dog or bitch that they are ready and willing, and it is not easy to cure him of doing it.

The same treatment as for mounting should be carried out, but it will probably be more difficult to stop.

When one dog mounts another this is not necessarily sexual – a

CAIRN CHARACTERISTICS

Mental stimulation is a must for the intelligent Cairn.

dominant dog mounts a subordinate to maintain superiority. Both males and females will do this.

COLOURS

Colours in Cairn puppies can be very deceptive, and can lead to many being called the wrong colour. Most are born with dark baby fluff which, with plenty of brushing and combing, comes out at about 12 weeks old. The actual colour will then be seen. An experienced breeder will usually be able to tell what colour a puppy will be; breeders with less experience find it more difficult.

The accepted colours of Cairns are Cream (the colour of cream), Wheaten (the colour of wheat), Red (a golden fawn) and Grey (light grey to dark grey), with brindling in all colours. Brindle is where black hairs mingle with the base colour. Brindle Cairns usually darken with every moult, and by the time they are five or six years old, may appear very dark grey.

A Wheaten or Red Cairn may lighten with age, the undercoat staying a brighter colour than the topcoat. The reason for these colour changes is unknown, but they are quite normal. It is rare for a Cairn to be mis-marked, but it is possible for a throwback from many, many generations ago to appear occasionally. Dark ears and masks are quite usual, and enhance the beauty and attractiveness of the Cairn. Some people have a preference for a particular colour, and, if the preference is strong, then it is better to wait until a puppy of the chosen colour is found than to have one that may be considered 'second best'. In most cases, colour is of secondary importance.

3 Choosing A Cairn Terrier

If you think a Cairn is the breed of dog that you would like, then it is wise to see some before making a firm decision. You may have a friend or acquaintance who has a Cairn, or you may be able to go to a dog show where Cairns are being exhibited, which is a good way of seeing the difference in the colours. You may meet a breeder who has, or knows of, some puppies available.

When you have seen as many Cairns as possible, and considered their characteristics and their suitability for your lifestyle, it may

Try to see as many Cairns as possible so you can decide on the type you like.

appear that buying one would be easy. This often proves to be a difficult problem.

As with most things, a personal recommendation is probably the safest way. If a friend has a healthy one with a good temperament, then an approach can be made to the breeder concerned.

No sensible breeder will promise you a puppy before the litter is born. They may not arrive safely, or they may not be the sex or colour you want. The breeder will probably want to keep the best one, or perhaps two.

Most Cairn Terrier Clubs keep a list of any of their members with puppies available, and will forward their names to anyone wishing to buy a puppy.

The buyer does not need to be a member of any club. It is a free service, but it is not a recommendation. It is up to the buyer to assess whether they wish to purchase a puppy from that particular breeder.

If you buy a Cairn puppy through one of the Cairn Breed Clubs, it means that the breeder belongs to a Cairn Club and is probably known to other Cairn breeders. Your national Kennel Club can provide a list of Cairn Terrier Clubs.

MEETING THE BREEDER

When you have located a breeder who has (or will have) a puppy for sale, it is wise to ask if you may go to see the family of Cairns before deciding to buy. On arrival, note the general appearance of the premises. Do they appear to be a commercial establishment with several breeds available, or a private house where the Cairns are treated as family?

Not all properties are kept in pristine condition, but does everywhere appear to be looked after to a reasonable degree? Consider whether you would buy anything from a shop that looked run-down, unkempt and scruffy. The premises should not smell of anything, whether it be an overpowering doggy smell or a strong disinfectant smell that may have been sprayed around to disguise other smells just before your arrival.

Do not be dazzled by rows of rosettes on the wall – they may indicate excellent wins, but they may have been won where there was no competition or in a 'fun' class.

If possible, see where the dogs are kept, even if it is at a distance. How much room do they have? Cairns are very active and need to have space to run and chase. Are they kept on concrete? Concrete needs to be disinfected regularly, which leaves it damp and cold. A bare run is similar to imprisonment, even if it is hygienic.

Has the breeder questioned you as to your suitability as a Cairn owner – whether your garden is secure and whether you have time to make a friend of the puppy?

Responsible breeders do not sell puppies to anyone unless there is someone at home for most of the day. No-one would expect you to

always be at home, every hour of every day – obviously, everyone has to go out at times, and a puppy should be able to be left for an hour or two. However, for anyone who goes to work all day, a Cairn is not suitable.

VIEWING THE PUPPIES

When you have located some Cairn puppies, ask to see the litter when they are about five weeks old. This has several advantages – you can see the complete litter, and you can see how they are kept. You can see how the mother

The puppies should be bright-eyed, clean, and inquisitive.

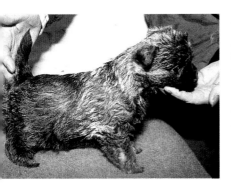

The breeder will help you to assess the finer points if you are looking for show potential.

looks – if it is a large litter, she may be rather slim, but she should have been fed well enough for her not to look 'pulled down' and weary. You will probably not be allowed to see the babies before they are five weeks old – the mother may become upset if strangers are around, the puppies will sleep for most of the time and, to your eyes, they may be indistinguishable anyway.

It is important to see the mother with her babies. That will tell you that the puppies are actually hers. Be suspicious if you are told that there is any reason why she cannot be with them. It is rare for a Cairn mother to be excitable or sulky – they are usually sensible and tolerant, and enjoy playing with their babies. She should have somewhere that she can jump on to, where her puppies cannot reach her, but from where she can go to them whenever she wishes.

You may not be allowed to walk into wherever the puppies are kept, and you may not be allowed to touch them. This would not be a reflection on you personally, but, the younger the babies are, the less immunity to disease they have, and, although all your clothes may be perfectly clean, you cannot say the same for the streets you have just walked on.

It is natural to be enchanted when you first see a litter of Cairn puppies – they are lively, energetic, bright-eyed bundles of mischief, but they soon tire and can fall asleep quickly, so do not expect them to be on the go all the time. When they are awake, they should be alert and lively, and they should run around freely and easily. They should feel firm, but not fat, and they should not have a bloated look.

When you first see a Cairn puppy, his ears will probably be folded over, and you may think they are incorrect. It is rare for them not to become erect as he grows, but the age at which they do varies from about five weeks to five months of age. It often

PUPPY WATCHING

Watch the puppies playing together to get an idea of individual personalities.

happens that a Cairn puppy's ears go up and down when he is teething. Their baby coats may be fluffy or smooth – the reason for the difference is not known and it does not indicate how the adult coat will be. Most Cairn puppies will run straight up to anything or anyone new to them. If there is one that does not, it will be difficult for you to assess whether he is just a cautious, aloof puppy or whether he has a shy, nervous temperament.

The exact age at which a Cairn puppy is ready to leave its home varies slightly. Some are ready at eight weeks old, but ten weeks is probably better. Although Cairn puppies are robust and strong, they are small, and an extra week or two with their family can be beneficial. The mother will teach them good manners in a way that no human can; they learn to take their place among their siblings and they need to be as mature as possible to face the trauma of a new home.

BUYING A PUPPY

It will be difficult for you to know whether any puppy is the age the seller says he is. Unscrupulous puppy dealers buy in litters and are casual about facts. If you are told that you can choose any puppy you like, then this suggests that the litter was bred in the hopes of making money. A person who exhibits and breeds Cairns in an attempt to improve the breed will want to keep the best one or two themselves. This does not mean that the one you are offered is a poor specimen. Competition is strong in the show ring, and there are many small things that can prevent a Cairn winning. A knowledgeable breeder will be able to tell you why he/she is selling a certain puppy. Probably, the conformation is not quite what is wanted, but even if this is so, it is quite possible that the puppy will grow up to be a pleasing Cairn.

A breeder who has bred only one, or perhaps two, litters is often so pleased with them and considers all the puppies perfect. This, of course, is an impossibility – it is not easy to breed a top winner. There are faults in all dogs – the perfect one has not yet been bred. All puppies are charming, and to have seen them born, watched them grow, kept them clean, weaned them and spent a lot of time with them means the owner is naturally besotted with them. It takes quite a lot of

experience to be able to predict
how a puppy will develop.

PRICE

With some commodities one buys,
the price indicates the quality. This
is not so when buying a puppy.
Anyone can charge anything they
like. The most expensive will
probably be the puppy dealer who
buys any kind of puppy to sell at a
profit. Some breeders charge 'as
much as people will pay'. Some
will have discovered how much
time, money and effort is needed
to rear a litter, and will want the
puppies sold as soon as possible.
You may be given sales talk on
how wonderful the puppies are,
how the parents have won many
prizes, or what a superb pedigree
they have. If a Cairn puppy is very
promising, there will be plenty of
people in the dog game waiting to
buy him, in the unlikely event of
the breeder not keeping him.

At the other end of the scale,
there are breeders who think that
no-one is good enough to have
one of their babies, and will
charge an inflated price on the
assumption that the more that is
paid, the better home the puppy
will have. The average breeder will
charge an average price, so talk to
as many as possible, and compare
conditions and price. Do not feel
pressurised to buy – rely on your
own judgement.

DOCUMENTATION

When you collect your puppy, you
should be given his pedigree, a
diet sheet, the date of his last
worming, an inoculation
certificate (if the puppy has been
inoculated) and a registration

*The big day arrives when it
is time to collect your puppy.*

certificate (if the puppy is registered with your national Kennel Club). If you are not interested in exhibiting or breeding, then whether the puppy is registered or not makes no difference.

THE FIRST FEW DAYS

Arrange to collect your Cairn puppy as early in the morning as possible. This will give him some time to become accustomed to his new surroundings before you have to leave him for the night.

Keep him in the room where he is going to sleep. It would not be fair to him to have him in several different rooms during the day, and then, when bedtime comes, to expect him to sleep somewhere else. He would not have had any chance of knowing where he is or where his bed is. Try to have one member of the family with him all day, except when he is asleep.

The puppy should be played with, but not made too excited. He should be talked to, so that he gets to know new voices as quickly as possible. Remember that a Cairn is a small breed and this is probably the most traumatic time of his life. He is only a baby and has been taken from everything he has ever known –

his mother, his siblings and the humans he has known. He is bound to be lost and bewildered so it is up to you to make the transition as easy as possible for him. Do not have visitors to see the new puppy yet; they can come a little later. Think of everything from the puppy's point of view.

FEEDING

Be prepared to follow the breeder's diet sheet accurately for at least one or two weeks. If you then wish to change the diet, do so slowly by adding a small amount of the new food at first and gradually increasing the amount. Most breeders will give

The new puppy will feel bewildered when he first arrives in his new home.

you a little of the food the puppy has been used to so that there is no sudden change in his diet. Do not overfeed for the first few days – an overloaded tummy, plus the trauma of a new home and the change of environment, can cause a puppy to have an upset tummy. His motions should be firm and well formed.

BEDDING

A plastic kidney-shaped bed 24 ins (60 cms) long is very good, and will be big enough for him when he is adult. It will be very easy to keep clean, is almost indestructible and will last a lifetime. It may be chewed, but probably not to a great extent. It will be flat enough for a small puppy to get into and out of easily. It should be lined with newspaper underneath the bedding because it does not 'breathe', and may become damp.

A Cairn puppy is small, so fill the bed with plenty of bedding. Polyester veterinary bedding is very good, or a woollen blanket is satisfactory. A well-wrapped hot water bottle and a ticking clock may help your puppy to settle. The hot-water bottle gives the warmth that he was used to from his siblings, and the ticking clock is supposed to represent their heartbeats.

If these items are used, they must be very securely wrapped and put beneath the bedding. The hot water bottle would be dangerous if it was too near the puppy, as his skin is much more tender than that of humans. You may prefer to keep the room at summer temperature. A very dim nightlight may help, or perhaps a light left on in another room, giving just a little light.

INDOOR CRATE

It is a good idea to invest in an indoor crate for your puppy. This can be used for car travel as well as providing accommodation in the home. If you go and visit friends, you can take the crate with you, and your puppy will feel perfectly at home.

Most Cairn puppies soon become used to a crate. Put it on the floor with the door open, put his toys in it, and at mealtimes put his food in it. Let him go in and out of it for several days before you shut the door, and then shut it for only a few moments when he has found something he likes inside. Gradually lengthen the time the door is closed and you will probably find that your puppy

A plastic kidney-shaped bed lined with soft bedding is ideal for the new puppy.

regards it as his den and is quite happy in it.

Do not leave your puppy in his crate for long periods during the day – and never use it as a means of punishing your puppy.

HOUSE TRAINING

If your puppy has been newspaper -trained, you should place newspaper all around the room, but not in the middle. Even though he is only a baby, a Cairn who has been used to newspaper is intelligent enough to find it. Gradually use less paper until you only have it by the door, then outside the door (when you probably will not need any).

If he has not been used to newspaper, you may prefer to house-train without it. This can be achieved by watching him all the time and taking him into the garden frequently. At a very young age, he will not be able to wait. At about four or five months old, he should have control but some puppies take longer than others. Until a puppy has full control of his bladder he may wet with excitement, such as when meeting a stranger or being picked up.

If your puppy has an indoor crate, this can help to hasten house training. Divide the crate into sleeping accommodation, and place newspapers at the front of the crate. A dog does not like to foul his sleeping quarters, and so he will use the newspaper. Soon he will learn to wait until he is released from his crate and taken to the garden.

Whatever method of house training you adopt, your puppy should get used to relieving himself in the garden. You should carry him quietly and calmly, and praise him enthusiastically when he does oblige.

Some owners wish to train their puppy to urinate and defecate on command in a particular part of the garden. It is quite possible to train a Cairn to do this, but it needs careful thought first. The advantage is that the rest of the garden is never soiled.

The disadvantages are that the owner must be certain that the dog is able to get to that part of the garden for the next 15 years or so. If the owner moves house, the dog will have to be retrained to use another garden. He will not be able to go into boarding kennels, or to visit a friend's home. Someone will have to be at home to let him into the garden if you go out for the day.

The allotted part of the garden may become 'dog-tired' , making him reluctant to use it. Make sure that he does not have to wait when he wants to go, because this can lead to health problems in later life.

4 Caring For Your Cairn

From the moment your puppy arrives in his new home, you are responsible for all his needs. This can seem quite a daunting prospect but, fortunately, the Cairn is a hardy, adaptable little dog, and if you follow the following advice, there should be few problems.

CHOOSING A DIET

As a puppy, your Cairn will need four meals a day. The range of his diet will need to increase until he is taking a wide variety of foods.

As he grows, adjust the quantity of food you give him so that he is neither fat nor thin. Never allow him to become a fussy eater. A dog has far fewer taste buds than a human does and it is natural for him to eat quickly. If he does not, omit his next meal. If his motions are loose, you are probably overfeeding. The breeder may have given him goat's milk; if so, it is worth trying to obtain some.

Goat's milk will not have been treated, homogenised, pasteurised or sanitised in any way, and puppies usually thrive on it. Although advertisements indicate that certain additions to a diet are necessary, oversupplementation of vitamins and minerals does more harm than good. If you particularly wish to add something to your puppy's diet, give very small amounts, about one-eighth the amount for a human baby, once or twice a week.

The Cairn is naturally an omnivore and an opportunist, eating anything and everything that comes his way. In the natural way of living, dogs make a kill, eat the intestines first, then, if they are not really hungry, they will bury the meat and bones to allow them to ripen before eating them.

A general rule is, if you would eat the food yourself, then it is suitable for your Cairn. He thrives on a varied diet. Raw meat, raw

It is essential to feed a top-quality, balanced diet, particularly while your puppy is growing.

vegetables and fruit, and breakfast cereals or dried wholemeal bread, given in proportions of one third of each, is a good basic diet. When you give your raw vegetables or fruit, it is safest to slice them into long strips rather than chunks. In their eagerness to eat them, it has been known for Cairns to choke on chunks.

Wild dogs and wolves do not eat every day, and some sled dogs are fed only every few days to keep them fit for the hard work they have to do. The same amount of a balanced diet every day is neither necessary nor desirable. Varied amounts most days keep the appetite sharp.

There is a plethora of commercial dog foods on the market. Many suggest that only human-grade food is used. A brief pause for thought makes one realise that the parts that humans eat will not be used for dog food. Many dogs live all their lives on manufactured food. A 'middle of the range' food is best suited to the Cairn. Beware of too rich a diet and too many additives – they do more harm than good. If a varied diet is fed, there is no need for supplements, even though the multitude of advertisements suggests they are essential.

QUANTITIES

Many pet dogs are too fat, unable to gallop and play as they should. Most Cairns are gannets, always looking for something to eat, and always telling you that they are hungry. If your Cairn does not keep his head in his food bowl until he has licked it quite clean, then you are overfeeding. Reduce the amount and keep reducing it until he is eagerly waiting for his next meal. An exact amount cannot be given for any food or any dog. Like humans, some can eat a lot and stay quite slim, but others gain weight with a moderate amount. Much depends on the lifestyle that is led. If you cannot feel the ribs of your Cairn, he is too fat, but, if the ribs are sticking out, he is too thin.

If your Cairn should become thin for any reason, perhaps after an illness or staying in kennels,

Although it is small in stature, the Cairn is an active breed and should never be allowed to become obese.

you will naturally increase his food for him to regain his normal weight. Rather than give larger quantities, it is better to give several smaller meals. Four meals a day are very suitable – they can be as varied as you like, or as varied as he likes. A cheese sandwich is often eaten with relish, but ensure that the bread is wholemeal and that butter is used, not margarine. Breakfast cereal and full-cream milk make another easily prepared meal, which is wholesome and often enjoyed.

NATURAL DIET

Cairns will eat grass and roots of grass. They should never be prevented from doing so – they know what they need better than their owners. Most will take fruit from shrubs – raspberries, currants, gooseberries, apples, pears etc. They will also dig their own vegetables, such as carrots, if they can get into a vegetable garden. None of these are washed and are quite natural for a dog.

Even though they are well fed, have fresh water to drink, have owners who ensure that all their food, water and bowls are clean and hygienic, when they are out for a walk Cairns will still scavenge and eat food that has been discarded for some time. They will drink from muddy puddles that doubtless have thriving microscopic life swimming around in them. They will eagerly eat garden compost, which contains millions of tiny creatures too small to be seen with the naked eye.

By doing these things they are probably fulfilling a basic need and rarely have any tummy upsets afterwards, providing they do not ingest any chemicals.

COPROPHAGIA

Sometimes dogs will eat their own or other dogs' droppings – this is called coprophagia. This, to humans, is extremely objectionable, and, at present, the reason they do it has not been discovered.

Several theories have been put forward – that they are bored; that they wish to 'keep their surroundings clean'; that it is just a bad habit; that they are lacking something in their diet; and that it is quite natural. The last two theories are the most probable. Giving pineapple, raw or canned, seems to prevent them doing it.

There are some animals (including rabbits and chimpanzees) that pass partly digested food and eat it, thus giving them vitamins that are not available in fresh food. Maybe the dog does so too.

GROOMING

Your Cairn should be trained to accept some grooming as a puppy. Some Cairns prefer not to be groomed, but, if it is done very gradually and without any stress, your puppy will soon become used to it. He must be brushed and combed; this is easiest if you have him on your knee at first.

A Cairn has a 'double coat' – a harsh outer coat and short, soft undercoat. If he is brushed with a very stiff bristle brush and combed with a steel comb every day, or every other day, his coat will not shed and the few hairs that come out will not cling to clothes or furnishings.

A Cairn's coat may become long and shaggy, which makes him look tatty and uncared-for. He may then be taken to the grooming parlour, where he will probably be bathed and his coat taken off with clippers. This is preferable to allowing him to become unkempt, but, in time, it will spoil his natural, harsh coat.

It is better for the owner to take out the long, dead hair – it is not difficult, but it does need a little practice. Any long, light-coloured dead hair should be plucked out with the finger and thumb. Some people think that this will hurt, but if the hair is dead and is pulled firmly in the direction that it is growing, there will be no discomfort. The aim should be to keep the coat about 2 ins (5 cms) long.

Some Cairns grow long hairs on the back of the ears, which spoil their smart, alert appearance. Remove a few hairs at a time by pulling with finger and thumb.

The only places scissors are used are around the feet and under the tummy. Care should be taken to ensure that the softer hairs on the tummy and armpits are kept free of knots and tangles by remembering to brush and comb them. This is easiest to do with the Cairn lying on his back on your knee.

Many people do not brush and comb thoroughly enough to keep a Cairn's coat in good condition. It is necessary to groom right down to the skin; the comb should not just glide over the top. He should first be brushed from tail to head – this will get rid of any dust in the coat and will help to remove dead hair. Then, brush the way the coat lies.

COAT CARE

The Cairn needs regular grooming to keep his coat in good order.

Long, dead hair can be plucked using finger and thumb.

The new coat can be seen once the dead hair has been removed.

Hair growing on the ears should be kept short.

A nice, tidy coat after grooming.

An older puppy will cast his coat when the puppy coat is dead, and this allows the adult coat to come through. A bitch will often cast her coat after a season and almost always after a litter.

NAILS
Nails will need trimming, and this can be done using an ordinary nail-file. It is a good idea if your puppy gets used to this procedure from an early stage.

You should note whether he has dewclaws. These are a little way up from the feet on the inside of the legs. They will probably be only on the front legs; if there is one on a back leg, it is preferable to have it removed by the vet. Dewclaws need to be trimmed regularly because they do not get any wear.

DENTAL CARE
Your puppy will change his teeth when he is four to six months old. You may find some of them on the floor, or you may never see them. When he is teething, his gums may be red and swollen, so be gentle when inspecting his mouth. Just like a human baby, he will need plenty of toys to chew. There is a variety of hard toys available.

A large hide chew is also

The dewclaw is located on the inside of the leg.

suitable – it softens as the puppy chews it, and, if he eats bits off it, they will not harm him. Do not buy small chews thinking that they are more suitable for a small dog – it has been known for a puppy to swallow one and for it to become stuck in his intestines.

Buy a chew about twice as long as the puppy – he will manage to drag it around and chew it quite well. It will last him a long time, but throw it away and buy a new one when it gets too small.

The age at which the ears of a Cairn puppy stand up varies from about five weeks to five months. It often happens that a puppy's ears go up and down when he is teething.

Big, strong teeth are one of the characteristics of the Cairn. He must have them cleaned, and an easy way to get him used to this while he is a puppy is to have something tasty on your finger and to rub it around his mouth. Later on, you can use an old soft toothbrush, or you can buy a

Teeth will need to be cleaned on a regular basis.

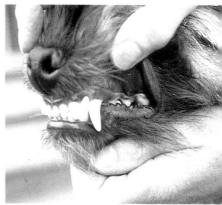

Large teeth, meeting in a scissor bite, are a characteristic of the breed.

'finger toothbrush' that you put on the end of your finger.

Your Cairn's teeth must not be left to accumulate tartar. Brush them two or three times a week; doggy toothpaste is available in various flavours. The alternative to keeping them clean yourself is an expensive visit to the vet.

BATHING

Your Cairn should never be bathed unless he has rolled in something objectionable! If he is bathed regularly, it will soften his coat and spoil its natural texture. The majority of Cairns live all their lives without having a bath; they do not smell if brushed and combed thoroughly. A Cairn that has been enjoying a good dig may have mud clinging to his face, legs and tummy. You can stand him in a bowl of water to clean the mud off and then dry him with towels or you can put several layers of newspaper in his pet carrier and put him in it in a warm room until he is dry. Then stand him on some more newspaper and brush him with a stiff brush; the soil will fall out and his coat will not need any more attention.

EXERCISE

A fit, adult Cairn can easily walk

The Cairn benefits from a daily walk.

five miles every day. Very few achieve this, but as much exercise as possible is beneficial. It is not good for man or dog to sit around all week and then go for a long hike at weekends. The aim should be a daily walk, plus games in the garden. A vigorous gallop helps to keep the body in good order. Most Cairns will chase a ball; this gives them pleasure and exercise. If a ball is thrown up a hill, the dog gets great benefit from running up and down it to retrieve the ball – but this does not help the owner's figure! It is important that the ball is large enough not to be swallowed. Deaths have been known to occur because a ball blocked the windpipe. The ball should be soft enough and of such a size that the Cairn can pick it up.

If you live in an area with somewhere your Cairn can run freely, this will greatly help to keep him fit and well. He is an active dog and he will run around and travel much farther than when he is on a lead. If you have nowhere to go where he can run off the lead, an extendable lead is very good when walking in a park or open space. It allows him a certain amount of freedom, but you still have control of him. They can be locked to a short length when you are on a busy road. Do not use one until your Cairn is trained to walk sensibly on a normal lead – it is impossible to train him unless you have full control over him.

FOULING
You should make yourself aware of the local laws on dogs. Dogs may be banned from certain areas but allowed in others. Rules regarding dogs are constantly altering, so you would be wise to have up-to-date knowledge of them.

In some areas, special bins for dog excreta are provided. It is possible to buy 'poop-scoops' for picking up any waste from your Cairn when you are out in public. You should always carry one of these, or a plastic bag, when you are out with him. The exercise of walking sometimes causes him to defecate and he should not be scolded for a natural occurrence. You can be fined if you do not clean up if your Cairn defecates in a public place.

IDENTIFICATION
To have an identification mark on your Cairn, he can be tattooed or microchipped. A tattoo is placed in the ear or the groin and can be easily seen by anyone, although sometimes they may fade.

A microchip is a small pellet inserted under the skin and has to be read by the appropriate reader for that particular type of chip. They are not yet universal or perfected; they can occasionally move around the body and can cause irritation when near electrical appliances. Obviously, tattooing or microchipping is done commercially and has to be paid for, but, if your Cairn should become lost, there is more hope of recovering him if he is identified.

All dogs need to wear an

If you keep two dogs, they will get plenty of exercise just playing together.

identity tag when they are in public. This should have your address and/or phone number and the Cairn's name on it. It is also a good idea to have the words 'Cairn Terrier' added, because, if your Cairn did become lost and you phoned the police, it is more than likely that they would not know what a Cairn looks like.

WELFARE

Cairn Terriers are very fortunate in having excellent welfare services – The Cairn Terrier Relief Fund in the UK, the Cairn Rescue Network in the USA, and European countries with their own organisations.

In all cases, welfare workers give their time to help any Cairn in need of re-homing. They are willing to help if the owner is not able to keep the Cairn through death, illness, hospitalisation or having to relocate to accommodation where dogs are not allowed.

If you are unable to continue to look after your Cairn and wish to have him re-homed, you will be asked to sign a form relinquishing ownership. Fortunately, Cairns are so suitable as family pets that there is usually a waiting list of people wishing to adopt one.

5 *Training Your Cairn*

Whether you realise it or not, you will begin to train your new puppy as soon as he arrives at your home. This should not be formal training – that should come later, and be introduced very gradually – but from day one you can have a sensible attitude towards him.

In a pack of dogs there is one pack leader. In a home environment the owner must take that role. If the owner is a weak person who is not consistent, the puppy soon realises it. As he grows, it may be in his nature to take advantage of any weakness of character and he may try to dominate the owner. This

The Cairn is a bright, intelligent dog who will benefit from training.

The inquisitive Cairn will be fascinated by all new situations.

domination may be very slight and the owner may be quite happy with it.

The owner needs to be firm and fair – firm enough to let the puppy know that 'No' means 'No', and fair enough not to say 'No' unless the puppy has done something that is forbidden.

Dogs soon come to trust a firm and fair leader. Trust is essential for a successful relationship between dogs and humans. Your training when your Cairn is a puppy will last all his life. You will find that a Cairn is quick to learn and will soon learn bad or good habits, and that the bad ones can be corrected only with much skill and patience.

Most new owners make many plans about what they will, and will not, allow a puppy to do. This is quite a good idea, but it is doubtful if many of the rules will be adhered to. Cairns are well known for getting their own way, and many new owners are surprised at how quickly they work things out for themselves, sometimes ahead of their owner.

In one household the Cairn was not allowed on the chairs, and the owner was pleased with how well he complied with the rule. He could be left alone and was always on the floor when the owner returned. It was quite a long time before it was discovered that the chair was warm!

BE POSITIVE

Your first training should be 'positive' training, by using the word "Yes" encouragingly when the puppy does anything that you allow – eats his food, plays with his toys, goes to his bed. By repeating "Yes" when he is doing the desirable action anyway, he will soon learn what it means. He may not know that you wanted him to do it, but a Cairn will be intelligent enough to know that you are pleased with him. When praising him, speak in an excited, delighted, rather high-pitched voice. Dogs have a different hearing range to humans and cannot hear low voices.

Think ahead and avoid letting him get into situations where you will need to say "No" – that day will come soon enough! Obviously, your "No" should be spoken sharply, but not shouted. If it is not sufficient to prevent him doing what you do not allow, hold him firmly, show him the object he is not allowed, and repeat "No!"

BODY LANGUAGE

Dogs react to body language – they use it between themselves and understand it immediately. Your Cairn does not need to talk to ask another dog (or you) to play with him. He will go down on his front legs, have his ears up with a 'come on' expression on his face, bounce backwards and forwards, and he may bring a toy to play with.

If he is unsure of how he will be received, he will carry his tail and ears down and look apprehensive. If he is in a dominant situation, he will raise himself to his full height, tail and ears up, with the hair on his shoulders raised. These signs are easy for dogs or humans to recognise, and just as easy to copy, so use them as well as your voice when talking to your puppy.

If you are pleased with him, use body language by getting down to his level, perhaps clapping your hands in a pleased way or patting the floor to mimic his 'front legs down, rear legs up' posture. If you are cross with him, walk tall in a determined, irate manner, say "No" in an angry voice, then ignore him completely, slam the door on him and leave him alone. He will know what you mean.

TOYS AND GAMES

Toys provide a pet dog with mental and physical stimulation. There are many different toys for sale. Playing with a ball or a 'this-way-and-that-way' bouncing toy keeps a Cairn alert and agile, and provides excellent exercise. Balls should be soft enough to be picked up and large enough not to be swallowed – dogs can choke to death by having a ball lodged in the throat. Most Cairns like a tightly-rolled old sock – they often throw it in the air and then catch it.

To provide change, toys can be given on a rota basis, but sometimes a Cairn will become attached to a favourite toy and will like to have it with him all his life. Toys that squeak are enjoyed, but make sure the squeak cannot be removed and swallowed. Toys to chew, such as hard nylon or hide, provide exercise for teeth and gums and help to remove tartar.

Tug-of-war toys are not a good idea, although almost all dogs and humans enjoy them. Until the teeth are fully grown – about eighteen months old – playing tug-of-war games can move them. With an aggressive type of dog, the owner should always 'win' any game, but it is rare for the Cairn to show any aggression. He is intelligent enough to know what is fun and what is serious.

SOCIALISATION

Socialisation should begin as soon as your puppy has settled into his new home; carry him down the street for a short way. He will need to be carried firmly and securely and held close to your body so that he feels safe in your arms.

The safest way to carry a Cairn puppy is to have his rear on your hip and under your arm, your thumb on one of his shoulders, one finger between his front legs and your other fingers holding his other shoulder. This is not a thing that a child should be allowed to do – they do not have the experience to know how firmly to hold a puppy without crushing him. The puppy may wriggle, and a child could not control him.

By carrying the puppy wherever and whenever you can, he will become accustomed to different sounds and sights so that he will be more confident later. It will probably be some weeks before the vet allows him to meet other dogs or people, and, as a baby, he will be too young to be lead-

The well-socialised puppy will mature into an adaptable adult.

trained. Gradually lengthen the time and increase the places that you carry him.

When the vet allows him to mix with other dogs and to go out in public, try to find a 'puppy party' for him to attend. They are an excellent way of the puppy becoming used to mixing with other puppies and their owners.

If there is any training connected with a puppy party, it should be minimal at first. For the puppy to build his confidence and to learn to trust other dogs and humans should be the aim. Having a rough-and-tumble with other puppies also teaches puppy that he cannot have all his own way. A Cairn can play with a larger breed without coming to any harm.

A Cairn puppy grows and develops quickly – not like some breeds, which have a lengthy babyhood and do not understand what is required of them. If you are a firm and fair owner and do not expect a baby to be an adult, you will find that a very young Cairn knows what you want and will try to please, even though he will be full of fun and mischief.

As a breed, Cairns are brave little dogs, but, in the same way that some children dislike certain situations, there may be those which your Cairn dislikes. He needs to encounter as many different situations as possible while he is young.

It may happen that he is frightened by something, say, for example, a car. If he is, do not fuss or say "It's alright, it won't hurt you", because that would only be reinforcing the fear in his mind. On the other hand, do not 'run away' from the fear. It is up to you to give him confidence.

In some instances, it may be necessary to pick your dog up and remove him from the situation, but try to act as though you did not know he was afraid. For example, you could say "I think we will go and see what is this way", and keep talking in a conversational way – your voice will reassure him.

Think ahead and choose two or three places where he will be able to see cars at a safe distance. The following day, take him to one of them, wait around quietly, and let your puppy stand and stare. Keep talking about anything you like, but do not fuss. Over several days move very gradually nearer and nearer the car. It may take some time before your puppy is confident enough to go near them, but with patience, that day will come.

CAIRNS AND CHILDREN

Children should not be expected to train a Cairn; they can help, under the supervision of an adult, but they are not consistent enough to undertake it by themselves.

Small children should not be allowed to try to groom a wriggling puppy – this could well lead to accidents. A Cairn is small enough and adaptable enough for children's make-believe games. Some will be quite happy to be a little girl's 'baby' and to be pushed around in a pram. Most will enjoy a rough-and-tumble game on the floor, but the child must never be allowed to tease. Often a Cairn will play soccer. Whatever the game, it is essential that it is all done in fun and that the child is never spiteful in any way, intentionally or accidentally.

Children brought up with a Cairn as part of the family invariably remember the things they used to do together all their lives. A Cairn is patient enough to listen to all their troubles, give them a few licks to tell them he understands and then be ready to have some fun. Although he is small, a Cairn is tough enough for all members of the family to enjoy, and he often treats each member in a different way.

A small child should never be left alone with any dog. Dogs have different vision to humans and what may appear to be a normal gesture to us may appear as a threatening gesture to a dog.

TRAINING EXERCISES

Your Cairn puppy will need to learn some basic obedience excercises. Remember to keep

The well-behaved Cairn should walk on a loose lead, without pulling ahead or dragging behind. Photo: McGovern.

training sessions short, and give plenty of praise for good behaviour.

COLLAR AND LEAD TRAINING

Your puppy probably will not be used to wearing a collar. Some do not mind one and accept it straight away, and others hate them. To accustom him to having something around his neck, put a

TRAINING EXERCISES

Food rewards work wonders when you are training. A treat held above will result in a Sit.

The Stand is important if you are training a show prospect.

When teaching the Down command, lower the treat towards the ground.

The Stay should be built up in easy stages.

TRAINING EXERCISES

Most important of all, give plenty of praise during training sessions.

piece of wool on him and run your fingers around it when you are talking to him. Do not leave the wool or a collar on when you are not with him.

When you buy a collar for him, a rolled leather one is best for a Cairn – it will not damage the coat on his neck. For an adult, one of 16 ins (40 cms) total length is suitable. A collar should fit tightly enough so that it will not come over his head, and loosely enough so that you can run two of your fingers around inside it.

Training your puppy to walk on a lead is not difficult if it is taken very gradually. Before you want to put a lead on him, accustom him to walking with you. First of all, give him tiny treats from your hand. Next, when he is hungry, give him a treat that is just out of his reach so that he has to walk one or two paces to get it.

Gradually lengthen the distance he has to walk to get his treat. When he knows he will get his treat by following you the length of a room, slip a piece of light string under his collar and hold both ends. At first do not allow it to become taut – release it before he feels its pressure. Continue giving treats, but make the distances between each one longer and longer. Do not have any battles; if he does not want to follow you, finish training by doing something else and try again when he is hungrier.

When you are training your puppy to a lead, it is a good idea to train him to walk on your left. Do this by always putting yourself on his right, not by moving him, which could confuse him. If you should wish to exhibit him later, he will already be happy walking on your left. If your puppy is trained this way, he should not pull when on the lead.

A Cairn that pulls when out for a walk is no pleasure to himself or his owner. His bad movement will soon become fixed. If he does begin to pull, you should say "No", jerk the lead quickly to pull him back, and then let it go immediately. He will not like this, and after a few times he should stop pulling. Never pull on the lead yourself – that would achieve nothing. A quick 'jerk and let go' at the first sign of pulling will correct him.

OFF THE LEAD

To help to train him not to run away, kneel down, call his name, and, if he comes, praise him and pet him. Give him a treat sometimes, but not always. When the vet allows him out in public, take him to the largest open space you can find, put him down without a lead on, and walk away.

Your puppy will doubtless run around excited at the new smells and surroundings, but keep walking away. He will soon realise he is by himself and come to you. Praise him enthusiastically and continue walking. You are his pack leader, his family and his only source of security; he is a baby and not confident enough to stay by himself in strange surroundings.

Never scold a puppy for coming to you, however cross you are with him. He will have accepted you as his pack leader and will look to you for leadership. Never destroy his trust in you.

CAR TRAVEL

When the puppy is quite used to his pet carrier, train him to ride in a car. It is easiest if a passenger can sit on the back seat to note his reaction, but not to fuss him.

Most Cairns are quite happy to

travel, but, as with humans, some get car-sick or stressed. If either of these should happen, put him in his pet carrier in the car, but do not have the engine running. When he is used to that, start the engine but do not move the car. The next step is to drive the car a few yards and very gradually lengthen the distance.

It is often the movement of the car and the visual movement combining to produce a conflict that causes car-sickness. If possible, put a screen on the window that the puppy is facing, and, if the carrier is an open one, cover it with a light cloth. Always ensure that your puppy has plenty of air – never enclose him completely, as he can quickly become overheated and die.

Sensible precautions should be taken when your Cairn is travelling in the car. He can easily jump around and so he should be confined in some way. There is always the possibility of the car stopping suddenly, when he would be thrown about. A dog's seat harness or a pet carrier will keep him restrained, but allow him sufficient room for movement for him to be comfortable. If there should be an accident, he will probably remain safe in his carrier,

The safest way to transport your dog is in a crate.

but he will be unable to undo his seat belt. Even reliable Cairns who always jump straight in or out of the car have been known to be attracted to something new and to dash to investigate it.

It may be necessary for you to open the car door when you are on a busy road, and he may think that he is allowed to jump out. Obviously, the result could be disastrous.

Never leave your Cairn in a car if there is any possibility of the sun shining. Do not make the mistake of thinking that, as he is a small dog, leaving a window or sun roof open will keep him cool

Allow your puppy to enjoy his growing-up period, and with firm, fair and consistent training, he will become a well-behaved adult who is a pleasure to own.

enough. The inside of a car heats up very quickly, even though it may be quite cool outside. Dogs do not perspire as humans do, and their bodies heat up much quicker.

The only way a dog can lose heat is by panting. If he becomes overheated, he will go into shock, and, unless treated immediately, he will die. This can also happen if he is outside in the sun without sufficient shade. Puppies and older dogs are most susceptible. If you discover a dog distressed by the heat, the quickest way to treat him is to plunge him into cold water. If this is not possible, pouring cold water over him will help, or packing ice packs (or frozen food) around him will bring his temperature down. Call a vet as soon as possible.

MOUTHING

Puppies of any breed should be trained to 'mouth' their owner's hand without marking it. This is important with a Cairn, who has strong teeth with a good bite.

For the first few days, avoid putting your hand by his mouth – keep giving him toys instead. This training should be done as soon as he is settled – his teeth are as sharp as needles and can rip your skin. It is inborn in his nature to bite and hold on to his prey, and he will treat anything that he can catch as prey.

Children should never be allowed to attempt this part of training. Allow your puppy to take your hand, but as soon as he tries to chew or bite it, push your hand towards his throat very firmly and say "No". He will not like a large hand in his mouth. Your instinct will be to snatch your hand away, but, if you do, his instinct will be to hold tighter and your skin may be torn.

If your Cairn puppy makes any attempt to chew or bite your hand, it is important that this lesson is learned as soon as possible. He will soon get to know how gentle he has to be. If he has suitable toys to chew and you keep saying "Yes" when he has one, he will soon know what is allowed.

If your puppy gets hold of anything that you do not wish him to have, never try to snatch it from him. This will make him hold it tighter. Pick him up and you will find that he will probably release it.

The owner should also look at things from puppy's point of view; unless he is taught the difference, he will not know whether the slipper is an old one that he can have for a toy or a new one. It is quite easy to teach him which is which by giving him the old one and saying "Yes" encouragingly and showing him the new one and saying "No".

The younger the puppy, the longer it will take for such lessons to be learnt, and you must take account of his age.

BARKING

It is good for your Cairn to bark when the doorbell rings or when there are strangers around, but he should stop when told to. A Cairn has a deep, strong bark for his size, and very few people know what breed of dog is barking.

A dog that does not stop barking when told to is objectionable. Barking dogs are one of the main causes of aggravation between neighbours. Barking can usually be stopped by saying "Be quiet" in a very firm voice, ignoring him and doing something different. Do not go for the walk or continue preparing his food, or whatever the cause of the barking was, until he is quiet. This will have to be repeated several times. If he persists in barking, shut him away by himself, preferably in a place where he cannot see anything or anybody.

As a general rule, Cairns are not whining, whingeing dogs; they are self-sufficient enough to be left by themselves for short periods if trained to do so as puppies. An adult can be trained to be quiet when left alone, but it will take more time and patience.

Choose a time when there is only you and him in the room, and be occupied doing something that he is quite used to, such as reading or washing up. Without saying anything, looking at him or in any way indicating that anything is about to happen, go

through the door, shut it, and immediately return and carry on with whatever you were doing. Keep repeating this until he takes no notice of you leaving.

By doing this and maintaining an attitude that this is quite a normal thing to do, you are teaching him that everything is all right and that you always come back. When he is quite used to this, take two steps away when you go through the door. Very gradually increase the distance you go away, and in time he will accept that you will return.

JUMPING UP

You should not allow your Cairn to jump up at anyone. It is a natural greeting instinct for a friendly dog like a Cairn, who loves the company of humans, but it is not appreciated when you have visitors or when you are wearing your smart clothes. It is preferable if you never allow a puppy to jump up by always going down to his level to greet him.

If an older Cairn jumps up, the easiest way to stop him is to jerk your knee so that his face suddenly comes into contact with it, because of his size. He will not like it, but it will not harm him.

*A dog that jumps up is
not always appreciated.*

Being a Cairn, he may know better than to jump up at his owners, but will do so when a visitor arrives.

To prevent this, enlist the help of two or three doggy friends, invite them to visit and ask them to do the knee jerk as soon as he approaches them. Until you are proficient at it, you and your friends may need to practise!

PUPPY BEHAVIOUR

Do allow your puppy to act like a puppy – he will grow into an adult soon enough. He must fit into your way of life, but to expect a young puppy of, say, twelve weeks to walk to heel etc. is not necessary.

Like children, puppies develop at different ages. Providing that he is gradually learning what you are teaching, that his house training is improving and his food intake is increasing, things are satisfactory.

At five to six months old, he should walk on a lead without pulling, know his name and stop whatever he is doing when you say "No". If he is not improving, your methods are probably wrong. All training should be enjoyable for the owner and the puppy.

Think ahead and do everything very gradually with a puppy. Be fair and firm, make all training enjoyable and your Cairn will be happy and willing to please you.

6 *New Challenges*

The Cairn is an ideal companion, but for those who want to get more from owning a dog, there is a variety of opportunities available.

THE SHOW RING

Dog showing is not a hobby that everyone, human or canine, enjoys. There are, however, many successful breeders and exhibitors who had their first introduction to the world of dogs by showing their pet Cairn. There is much pleasure to be obtained from this pastime, but it is essential that you are prepared to lose as well as to win.

Most Cairns that are shown today belong to owners who have only a few dogs. At one time, there were large kennels with plenty of kennel staff. Cairns were favourites of the British aristocracy and the Royal family. Queen Victoria owned at least two, and the then Prince of Wales had a Cairn, which won a Reserve Bitch Challenge Certificate at the Caledonian Canine Society's Championship Show on January 1st 1924.

Showing dogs today is an expensive hobby, but possibly no more so than some other hobbies. Plenty of stamina is needed; you need to be able to travel widely, to be prepared for all weathers and conditions, often to make very early morning starts and, of course, to have a Cairn good enough to show. For most people there is more pleasure in showing a Cairn that they have bred themselves. There is no easy way to success in dogs; it takes patience and years of trial and error – and then you need that little bit of luck. Any breeder who sells a 'show puppy' either knows nothing about the development of dogs or is looking through rose-coloured glasses! Would you predict that a beautiful human

Crufts 1997

GROUP WINNER

The rewards of showing a top-quality dog – this is Ch. Kinkim Ludvic, handled by Ron Birch, winning the Terrier Group at Crufts.

baby would grow up to have the face, figure and personality to become a beauty queen? An experienced breeder may sell a puppy with 'show potential'.

Very occasionally, an unpromising puppy may develop into a pleasing, well-balanced adult.

There is a saying that dogs are like their owners. This is true in many cases; Cairn people on the whole are friendly and helpful, ready to smile and forgive. Many people have found that by showing their Cairn they have made true, lifelong friends. If a Cairn, or his owner, needs help, a call to the nearest exhibitor often results in immediate assistance being given, however inconvenient it may be.

PREPARATION

If training for shows starts when the Cairn is a baby puppy, he will grow up accepting it as part of life. At that age, everything should be done in a gentle, playful manner, without any strictness. Accustom the puppy to standing on a table by giving treats and moving your hands over him at the same time. Always have the puppy on your left when you take him for a walk.

The Cairn is not one of the trimmed terriers, and, although he is now smartened up for the show ring, he still resembles the original Cairn. The coat is always tidied by tweaking out long hairs with the finger and thumb to give the desired shape – scissors or knives are never used. It is not easy for a beginner to know how much coat to take out, and, if possible, you should try to find someone who will show you. If this is not possible, study photographs or go to see Cairns in the show ring, and remove just a few hairs at a time.

Your Cairn also needs to be in good condition, neither fat nor thin, and to have plenty of exercise. Without exercise, he may look good when he is standing, but he will not have the freedom of movement and suppleness that a Cairn should have. He ought not to toddle around the ring with effort.

TYPES OF SHOW

There are different levels of dog shows ranging from small, fairly informal events to the big General Championship Shows, at which many breeds are scheduled. A Championship Show is the only show where awards can be won towards becoming a Champion, the highest accolade of the dog show world.

Each breed is judged against its own Breed Standard, which is a written blueprint of the 'ideal' dog. It is the judge's job to assess all the entries and decide which dog comes closest to the Standard. Personal interpretation plays a part, and that is why the same dog does not win every show.

WHAT TO EXPECT

At present, the number of Cairns being shown is about halfway between the breeds that have huge entries and those with small entries. This is quite pleasing; it means that Cairns are not too popular, but that there are enough competitors for competition to be strong.

The judge will examine each dog to assess conformation and temperament.

Each entry is 'gaited' for the judge. When the dog is moving, the expert can evaluate how it is put together.

A Cairn is shown 'free-standing' – that is, standing naturally on a loose lead, not having each leg placed by the exhibitor or having his head and tail held. Practices such as these can help to disguise faults a dog may have, and in this way a Cairn is at a disadvantage, but it would be most displeasing to see a Cairn standing like a statue. Even though he is shown in as natural a way as possible, before taking your Cairn to a show, he needs some training. You may be able to find ring training classes near your home; these can be helpful in accustoming you and your Cairn to the show world.

Mini-Agility is a fun sport for both dog and owner.

Your Cairn will be expected to stand on a table while the judge examines his conformation by feeling all parts of his body and looking at his teeth. The judge will also want to watch your Cairn on the move. It is the dog's movement the judge wishes to see, not yours, so the dog walks on your left around the ring.

Your Cairn should also stand sensibly when the other dogs are being examined, and you should be ready to attract his attention to make him bright and alert whenever the judge looks at him. If you are a beginner, it may be mystifying why you can win one week and not the next. Even if you have been able to buy a really good Cairn, and you show him well, he may not always win. Judges are at liberty to place the dogs however they wish. This is one reason why dog showing is not really a good hobby for children.

The cheerful nature of the Cairn makes an ideal therapy dog.

AGILITY AND OBEDIENCE

Your Cairn can also compete in Agility or Obedience. He may not be an excellent specimen of the breed, but he will almost certainly enjoy such shows. He will have something to keep his mind occupied and both he and you will get much pleasure from competing.

There are Cairns who have started Agility or Obedience when they have been six or more years old, so do not think that he is too old to learn. It may be that the Cairn, being a terrier, will not get to the highest level, but both he and you will have a lot of fun.

For children and teenagers in the UK, there is a Junior Handling Association where competitors are assessed on their skill at handling dogs. This may sound easy, but, in the advanced classes a high standard is needed. Junior Handling is one sport where all contestants are polite, well dressed and good losers.

THERAPY DOGS

While not classed as a show activity, another area where the Cairn excels is in being a Therapy Dog, known as Pets As Therapy (PAT) dogs in the UK. Your local breed club should be able to put you in touch with the appropriate organisation.

Owners take their dogs to visit people in hospitals, nursing homes or residential homes, where contact with a dog often helps patients to smile again. Obviously, to do this, a Cairn must be under control and be prepared to interact with people who are not too active, but who enjoy the bright cheerfulness of a Cairn.

7 Breeding Cairns

If you have your Cairn bitch as a companion, it is better if she does not have puppies. There is no truth to the old saying that it is good for her to have one litter. Breeding is not something to be entered into lightly, and, before deciding to have your bitch mated, there are several things to think about.

Breeding means a lot of work, a lot of time, a lot of money and probably a lot of worry. It also means being at home for at least twelve weeks – two weeks before the bitch is due and ten weeks before the puppies are sold. Someone who is not well known in the breed will probably have to advertise to sell the puppies, and it may be several weeks before a suitable buyer is found.

The cost of having a litter should be thought about. Add up the stud fee, extra food and heat, visits to the vet, a Caesarean section (if it should be necessary) and, if the worst happens and the bitch dies, the cost of her replacement.

Cairns do not have an exaggerated shape, and, if she is in good condition and has had plenty of exercise, a Cairn bitch will usually whelp without any problem. An experienced breeder knows when all is well or not well; an inexperienced breeder will probably have to make several visits to the vet.

Although not a big breed, the testicles of a male Cairn are usually descended by the time he is twelve weeks old. An adult male with no testicles descended is commonly called a cryptorchid. He cannot sire puppies. A male with only one testicle descended is commonly called a monorchid. He is able to sire puppies, but should never be used for breeding as the fault will be passed on, and females can pass on this fault as well as males.

The stud dog you choose must be an outstanding specimen of the breed, and must combine well with your bitch's bloodlines.

BREEDING PRINCIPLES

It has been found that, with Cairns, line breeding produces the best results. Line breeding is where both parents are distantly related. Outcrossing is where the parents are not related.

Inbreeding, which is the mating of close relatives, should not be undertaken except by very experienced breeders who may occasionally do it for a particular reason.

Interbreeding is when dogs of different breeds are mated together – this is never practised nowadays, but was undertaken in the formation of some breeds and used to be allowed between Cairns and West Highland White Terriers until 1925.

THE BITCH

On average, a bitch comes 'in season', 'on heat' or 'in oestrus' every six months. Cairns vary a great deal – some are very regular and always on time, some are early, some are late, and some are on time one season, but late another.

A season lasts for a three-to

four-week period, the middle of which is the optimum time she will accept the male. Some bitches will mate at any time of their season. When not in season, a bitch is not sexually interested in males or interesting to them. A bitch has seasons all her life – in old age they may become irregular and infrequent but she will doubtless be willing to mate. Males continue to be sexually active and capable of siring puppies all their life. A male Cairn will be prepared to mate with any bitch of any breed if she is in season.

Write down the date of your bitch's first day in season, and keep her firmly on a lead when you are out. Ensure that she cannot escape, and ensure that a male cannot get in. There are many, many incredible stories of bitches getting out of so-called secure homes and gardens, and

The bitch must be sound in mind and body, and must be fully fit before mating.

even more incredible stories of males getting in! Remember that Cairns are agile.

One male Cairn was seen balancing precariously on top of a five-foot high wooden fence in an attempt to get to a bitch in season. The owner never worked out how he managed to get there!

About eight to twelve weeks after she has been in season, a bitch may have a false, phantom or pseudo-pregnancy, even though she was not mated. Her hormones tell her that it is the time she would have had babies if she was pregnant.

Cairns are not as prone to having phantom pregnancies as some breeds. It is not an illness and should not be treated as such. It occurs in wolves and wild dogs when the unmated bitch provides milk for the alpha bitch's puppies.

PREGNANCY

After mating, most Cairn bitches carry on with their usual lifestyle for the first four to five weeks – eating, running, jumping and playing normally. It will be almost impossible to know if she is in whelp or not, although you will probably be very eager to know.

There is a theory that, if she is pregnant, she will finish her season earlier than if she is not. As some bitches have longer seasons than others, that theory can only be a guide.

Another theory is that, two days after mating, her discharge will be dark red in colour if she is in whelp. A frequent careful watch would have to be kept to notice any change in colour. Another is that her nipples will become pink – this will happen later at about the fifth week and is caused by increased blood flow, but at first it may not be noticeable.

Yet another theory is that at three to four weeks into pregnancy, there will be a slight change in her temperament – she may become more independent or she may want more fuss. She may have 'morning sickness', and not want to eat anything until evening. She may feel she cannot eat her normal food, and yet eat things she has never eaten before. Perhaps if she conforms to all these theories you can hope that she is in whelp.

If you possibly can, it is best if you forget that she has been mated for the first five weeks or so. She will not show much difference in her figure until then, when she may begin to lose her 'waistline'.

With a naturally active breed like a Cairn, it is important to keep to her usual exercise. At first there should be no difference, but, after the seventh week, be prepared to walk at her pace and for the distance that is comfortable for her.

PREPARING FOR WHELPING

If she were whelping in the natural way, a bitch would dig a hole in the earth, have her puppies there, and stay with them for two to three days before she came above ground to relieve herself and feed. You should provide a place where she will be by herself, be undisturbed and quiet.

An ordinary bed is not suitable for a whelping box. A wooden box of about 24 ins (61 cms) long and 18 ins (46 cms) wide with a hinged, or removable, front of 4 ins (10 cms) is suitable. The front should be removed when the puppies are about three weeks old – they will then stagger out to wet on the newspaper. Even at that young age, Cairns like to be clean.

The average gestation period for a bitch is nine weeks. Cairns often whelp at sixty-one days, but earlier or later whelpings have been known.

You should have everything ready by the time she is eight weeks pregnant; she should also be sleeping in her whelping box by this time. There should be no last-minute hustle and bustle.

WHELPING

There are signs to look for that will tell you when the birth is imminent. The bitch's vulva will enlarge in size, and muscles at the top of her back legs slacken. Her temperature will drop from the normal 101.5 degrees F (38.5 degrees C) to about 99.5 degrees F (37.5 degrees C) before she whelps. All these signs can become apparent just a few hours or as much as forty-eight hours before labour commences, so none of them can be taken as the only guide. The bitch will deliberately empty her bowels and bladder just before she starts labour – this is the most certain sign that she is about to start.

There are two golden rules when a bitch is whelping. One is to stay with her and the other is to write everything down. You may not have had any experience of whelping, but your common sense will tell you many things. It is fairly common for a Cairn to get out of her bed to produce a

THE DEVELOPING PUPPIES

For the first couple of weeks, the puppies will divide their time between eating and sleeping.

The puppies become increasingly boisterous.

By eight weeks of age it is time for the puppies to go to their new homes.

puppy, but obviously you would not leave it lying on a cold floor. If she is resting, you would not disturb her, and you cannot do anything to hurry the process.

THE NEW PUPPIES

It is essential that puppies receive the colostrum – the first milk – that the bitch has for two days after whelping. Bitches cannot transfer immunity from disease to their puppies before they are born, so they obtain it from the colostrum.

Puppies begin to hear at about ten days of age, and you may have read that eyes open at ten days. Perhaps that is common in some breeds, but some Cairn puppies do not open theirs until they are 16 days old.

The hardest thing about breeding puppies is letting them go to their new homes.

PREVENTING BREEDING

To prevent a Cairn bitch from breeding, the vet can give her injections to forestall her coming into season. This may cause womb problems at a later date, particularly if you wish to breed from her later. It may be more convenient to have her spayed, which is an operation to surgically remove her womb. Cairns are tough and phlegmatic, and providing she is fit and well before the operation, she will probably recover very quickly. The vet will probably ask you not to let her jump until the stitches have been removed.

The advantages are that she will not come in season, develop pyometra of the womb or have false pregnancies, and it is very unlikely that she will have mammary tumours. Spayed bitches usually live longer. The disadvantage is that, as with any operation, it costs money. To ensure that the bitch's female hormones are complete, it is often recommended that she should have one season before being spayed, and that spaying is done midway between seasons.

Castration is an operation to remove the testicles of a male. The advantages are that he will not be able to breed, although he may still show some interest if a female is very enticing when she is at the height of her season. If he is the type of dog that would like to be dominant, he will become more docile and he will be less likely to indulge in territorial marking. He will not develop cancer of the testicles. He will be less inclined to roam – entire males know when a bitch is in season, even though she may not leave her home. As with a bitch, the operation has to be paid for, but castration is not as expensive as spaying.

A neutered dog or bitch cannot add to the thousands of unplanned, unwanted puppies that are born each year. Some people say that a neutered Cairn will become fat, but this is not necessarily so. A dog becomes fat when he has too much to eat and not enough exercise. Many Therapy Dog organisations (such as Guide Dogs for the Blind, Hearing Dogs for the Deaf, Support Dogs and Dogs for the Disabled) use neuters; they are not fat, nor has their temperament been changed.

In most ways, it is fortunate that Cairns are a natural type of dog, but sometimes it is not very convenient. In some bitches, the urge to reproduce is so strong that, at the height of her season, she will try desperately to escape to find a mate. Cairn bitches have been known to dart through a door that has only been opened a fraction and much care needs to be taken to ensure that she is confined but treated as normally as possible.

If, in spite of being very careful, your bitch escapes and is mated, or if you suspect she has been mated, take her to the vet straight away so she can have a 'morning-after' injection. She will probably come in season again a few weeks later and greater care will need to be taken.

8 Health Care

Cairns are generally healthy dogs, often living well into their teens. Like all living things, they can become ill, and suffer from generally the same health problems as humans – diabetes, cancer, diseases of the liver, kidney, heart, eyes, skin, etc.

Fortunately, as there is quite a large gene pool in Cairns, there is nothing rife within the breed. All breeds, and mongrels, can suffer from hereditary problems, but at present there has not been sufficient research to prove, or disprove, how conditions are passed on. Perhaps, one day, all health problems in all mammals will be solved.

Do not be concerned if your Cairn's nose is hot and dry. When he is asleep or resting, his nose is

usually dry. When he is awake and active, his nose should be damp and cold. If he is less energetic than usual, seems unwell and has a dry nose, then it may indicate a temperature. To take a dog's temperature, a greased thermometer is inserted into the rectum. A sick dog rests more comfortably in a darkened room. Write down everything he does; if he becomes seriously ill, it may help the vet to know all the details.

If your Cairn has been ill and has had to have a course of antibiotics, it is helpful to feed some live yoghurt – it will help to restore the natural harmless bacteria that the antibiotics have probably killed.

VETERINARY SUPPORT

Before you buy your Cairn it is wise to approach a veterinary practice to make yourself known before you have your puppy at home. Most vets like to meet a new puppy, and, while this is a good idea, it is also wise to try to make the first visit as brief as possible. If your puppy has recently left his mother, his siblings, and the only home and people he has ever known, he is under stress. He should not be

expected to spend time in a waiting room full of other dogs and members of the public.

Most people go to the vet nearest to their home. This has much to recommend it, and, in case of an emergency, time can be very important. If you have more than one veterinary practice near your home, you probably will not know which to choose. The only criteria are how efficient and helpful the staff are when you first call, and the general appearance of the premises.

The qualifications of vets may appear confusing but, apart from specialists, the letters after their names usually reflect where they did their training.

VACCINATION

The age at which vets inoculate puppies varies, but generally the first injection is given at eight weeks old, with a second at twelve weeks.

Many Cairn breeders do not sell their puppies until they have had the first injection. Although this does gives the puppy some immunity against disease, you will need to keep him away from other dogs and public places until the vet says it is safe. Another advantage in the puppy having had his first injection is that most vets examine a puppy before injecting him. Obviously, this is a general examination and not for any particular disease, but it does

mean that you know your puppy is apparently healthy.

Puppies are usually vaccinated against Distemper, Hardpad, Leptospirosis and Parvovirus. Until recently, annual boosters were considered essential, but, as with many things in the world of medicine, it is now questioned whether yearly boosters are necessary or desirable. Humans are inoculated in childhood but do not have boosters. Many boarding kennels, however, will not accept dogs unless they have had their boosters.

WORMS

It is unforgivable for any puppy, or adult dog, to be infested with worms – it is so easy to add medication to their food. Most puppies of any breed are born with roundworms; the breeder should have begun treatment to eliminate them, and the buyer should continue treatment until adulthood.

Your vet may provide medication, or you can buy some from a pet store. It is important to weigh your puppy to ensure that you give the correct dosage for his size. A Cairn puppy is very small, and to overdose him with worm medicine could make him ill. It is quite usual for puppies to have worms, but they acquire immunity to them as they grow up, and adults rarely have them.

It can be a good idea to worm adults once a year, but it is not a good idea to keep giving worm medicine unnecessarily. Any worms you see after giving medication will be dead and will be harmless – it is the eggs that you cannot see that may cause any problem.

Never worm a sick puppy even if you suspect he has worms – take him to the vet and let the vet decide what treatment he needs.

MANGE

It is rare for a Cairn to suffer from a skin complaint, but it is, of course, possible. If he scratches strongly enough to make his skin inflamed and to lose hair, he may have mange.

If mange (follicular or sarcoptic)

is suspected, you should take him to the vet straight away. It is difficult to distinguish between the two, but both are conditions for a vet to treat, and not for home treatment. A dog with mange may smell. A healthy Cairn does not smell; if he does, then it is either because he is dirty, has a skin disease, or his feeding is wrong.

When he is growing a new coat, a Cairn will sometimes scratch to remove the old one, which is no cause for concern.

FLEAS

All dogs may catch fleas, regardless of their breed, age, sex, or where they are kept, and Cairns are no exception. Fleas cause the dog to scratch and can set up irritation of the skin. If your Cairn scratches, look for tiny black specks on the skin.

If you find any, they will be flea dirt, and will not move around, as a flea will. Fleas like warmth and so are more common in summer, but they can breed all year round.

At a good flea-breeding time one female can produce 20 eggs a day.

Fleas do not like garlic. Garlic gets into every pore of the body and a dog that is fed some garlic, either raw or in tablet form, is unlikely to suffer from fleas. There are many flea powders, lotions and creams on the market, but those that are strong enough to kill fleas may be harmful to your Cairn.

UPSET STOMACHS

Cairns seem to have cast-iron stomachs – there is probably not a household with a Cairn where he has not emptied the rubbish bin at some time or other. The owner is worried and prepared for a tummy upset the following day, but all that happens is that chewed-up foil or bits of eggshell are passed. If, however, your Cairn has diarrhoea, withhold all food for 24 hours, and allow free access to water, to which a little honey can be added.

When he is better, the first meal should be very bland – chicken and rice boiled together and liquidised is suitable. If he still has diarrhoea after 24 hours, take him to the vet.

There is rarely any cause for concern if your Cairn eats grass and vomits it back with yellow bile, or he may vomit clear yellow bile if he is unable to find the grass he wants. Give him some charcoal tablets or biscuits, obtainable at most chemists, and miss a meal; if he still seems unwell take him to the vet.

POISONS

There are several household products that are poisonous to a dog. As a general guide, if you would not eat it, ensure that your Cairn cannot – he is very adept at opening doors or rubbish bins.

Some of the less obvious substances that a Cairn may get hold of, even if you think he will not be able to find them, are as follows: mushrooms; dark chocolate; drugs that have been prescribed for the owner or the dog; painkillers; the contraceptive pill; lead in wine bottle stoppers/wrappers; batteries; and plumbing materials.

Some flea collars, powders or shampoos contain organophosphates and carbamates. Some dogs are more sensitive than others to these and can become ill if they are used. Slug bait contains metaldehyde and is very dangerous. If you suspect that the Cairn has eaten any, take him to the vet immediately.

Symptoms of poisoning are very varied and can be difficult to diagnose. Drooling, tremors, lack of co-ordination and breathing difficulties are often signs. If any poisoning is suspected, take the dog and the packet or label to the vet as soon as possible.

CUTS AND SORES

One part of hydrogen peroxide diluted with five parts of water usually clears up minor cuts, sores or interdigital cysts and can also be used for cleaning teeth, but care must be taken not to let any get into the eyes. When used on a wound, hydrogen peroxide gives off oxygen, creating gas bubbles that help to remove pus or dead matter.

ALTERNATIVE MEDICINE

There is an increasing number of people turning to alternative medicine for themselves and their pets. To cater for the need, it is now possible for most people to consult a vet qualified in alternative medicine within reach of their home. If you wish to do this, it is necessary to have a referral letter from your own vet before an alternatively qualified vet can give treatment.

Alternative medicine includes herbal treatment, homeopathy, acupuncture, physiotherapy and faith-healing, among others. Homeopathy and herbal treatment are the two most popular.

There are several books on both subjects, and so it is possible for you to treat your own Cairn for simple conditions – but a warning must be made against using any treatment for too long. If there is no improvement within a few days, discontinue the treatment. For most problems, several remedies are given. Homeopathic and herbal treatments usually take longer than drugs to cure a problem.

A homeopathic vet can give preparations to protect against disease instead of conventional vaccination. There is an increasing number of boarding kennels who accept pets that have been protected in this way. Information and some advice are available on the Internet.

As a general rule, the initial consultation will take much longer than with a conventional vet and will be more expensive, but the treatment may be cheaper. Some pet insurance policies cover alternative treatment, so, if you plan to take out pet insurance, it is worthwhile checking on this point.

INSURANCE

All vets' bills are expensive, particularly if an illness has to be referred to a specialist. Some owners take out insurance to cover such emergencies. As with all insurance policies, you should read the small print carefully so that you know exactly what is covered. Note whether third party liability legal costs are included. Cairns are quick and dash out of doors, gates or cars before the owner is aware of it. If your dog should cause an accident, you could be liable for any damage.

Some owners put the amount of money the premiums would cost into a bank account of their own until they have built up a certain amount and keep that to offset any bills.

USEFUL DATA

Normal temperature: 38 to 39 degrees C (100.4 to 102.2 degrees F)

Normal pulse rate: 70 to 120 beats per minute.

Respiration: at rest-10 to 30 breaths per minute; when panting – 200 breaths per minute.

Average life span – 13 to 15 years.